WHAT IS A BIRD?

Ron Hirschi

photographs by
Galen Burrell

Walker and Company
New York

For Bud and Evelyn

First published in the United States of America in 1987 by the
Walker Publishing Company, Inc.

Library of Congress Cataloging-in-Publication Data

Hirschi, Ron.
    What is a bird? / Ron Hirschi . color photographs by Galen
Burrell.
    Summary: Depicts basic concepts about a bird, such as feathers,
flight, and eggs.
    1. Birds—Juvenile literature. [1. Birds.] I. Burrell, Galen,
ill. II. Title.
QL676.2.H568 1987
598—dc19   87-16834
ISBN 0-8027-6720-6
ISBN 0-8027-6721-4 (lib. bdg.)

Printed in Hong Kong

10 9 8 7 6 5 4 3 2 1

Book design by Laurie McBarnette

WHAT IS A BIRD?

Birds are eggs, waiting.

A bird is soft, warm feathers.

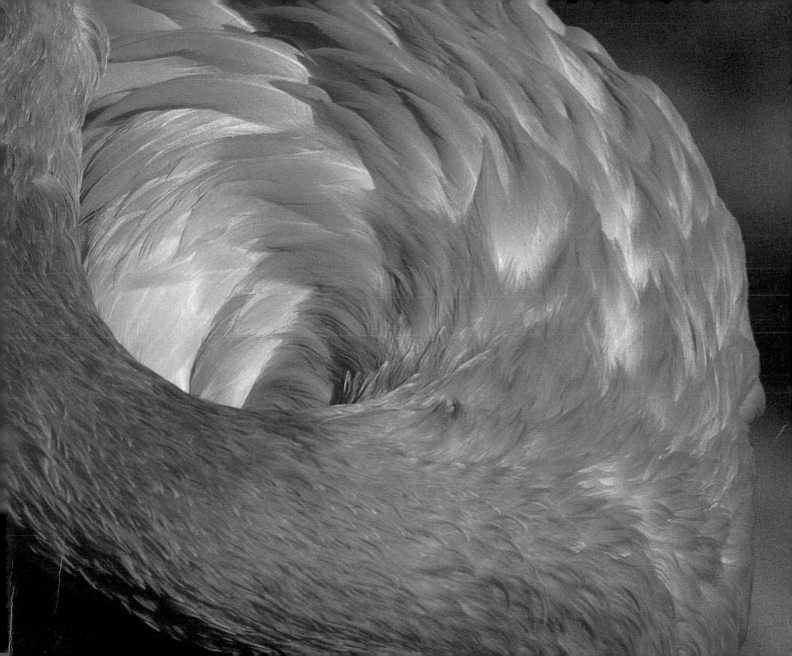

A bird is flight.

Birds balance on the wind,

or wire
or tiniest twig.

Birds leap.

Birds dive to catch a silver fish.

Birds dance a morning
dance.

Birds are red, yellow,

white and blue

Some sing a soft song and
hide from you.

Some sleep by day or by
night.

Each bird lives in its own home—its own all alone.

AFTERWORD

Birds are all these things and many more.
This introduction to their world is one way to share the wonder
of birds with young people. We hope that it will also encourage
them to express their own feelings and thoughtful concern for
birds and the world around us.

Cover: Yellow-headed Blackbird
Back cover: Flamingo
Frontispiece: Wood Duck

Page	Inset	Background
Eggs	American Coot	American Coot Eggs and Nest
Soft Feathers	Canada Goose	Flamingo
Flight	Trumpeter Swan	Snow Geese
Wind	Trumpeter Swan	Bald Eagle
Wire/Twig	Blue Grosbeak	Black-capped Chickadee
Leap	Gadwall	Sandhill Crane
Dive	Common Goldeneye	Pigeon Guillemot
Dance	Lesser Prairie Chicken	Lesser Prairie Chicken
Red/Yellow	American Goldfinch	Cardinal
White/Blue	White-tailed Ptarmigan	Mountain Bluebird
Soft Song	White-tailed Ptarmigan	Yellow-headed Blackbird
Sleep	Bar-headed Goose	Whistling Swans
Own Home	Great Egret	Red-winged Blackbird